alzheimer's  association®

the challenge your brain
PUZZLE BOOK

FEATURING PUZZLES FROM THE INTERNATIONALLY-SYNDICATED PUZZLE WRITER
TERRY STICKELS

Get ready to build your brain power!

The Alzheimer's Association is proud to share *The Challenge Your Brain Puzzle Book* with fans of *FRAME GAMES*,™ trivia and teasers across America.

Although this book is a perfect way to relax—on a train ride, at the airport or sitting in front of the TV—it serves another purpose as well. It's a fun and easy way to activate your brain, and it inspires you to learn more about Alzheimer's.

At the Alzheimer's Association, we want to help you maintain your brain. Although scientists are still working to unlock the mysteries of the body's most powerful organ, we do know there's a lot you can do to help keep your brain healthy as you age.

Challenge yourself to complete mentally stimulating activities. Remain socially active with friends and family. Exercise or adopt a hobby that helps you stay fit. Adopt a low-fat, low-cholesterol diet high in antioxidants. Together, these steps may reduce your risk of Alzheimer's disease or other types of dementia. You can get more tips on maintaining your brain health at *alz.org/maintainyourbrain*.

Currently, as many as 5.3 million Americans are living with Alzheimer's, and millions more are affected both emotionally and financially as they care for a loved one with the disease. Within this book you will find information about the 10 warning signs of Alzheimer's disease. If you or someone you care about is experiencing any of the 10 warning signs, please see a doctor to find the cause. Early diagnosis gives you a chance to seek treatment and plan for your future.

Now open this book, start having fun—and spread the word about Alzheimer's.

For more information about the 10 warning signs, please contact the Alzheimer's Association at 877-IS IT ALZ (877.474.8259) or visit www.alz.org/10signs.

Table of Contents

the **challenge** your **brain** PUZZLE BOOK

PUZZLE CATEGORY KEY:

CREATIVE THINKING: Thinking outside the box

MATHEMATICS: Computational skills

LOGIC: Analysis and deduction

LANGUAGE: Definitions, usage and sentence structure

VISUAL: Observation, spatial reasoning and pattern recognition

WORDPLAY: Word and letter manipulation

KNOWLEDGE: Book smarts and memory

alzheimer's ᑫᑭ association®

KNOW the
10 SIGNS
EARLY DETECTION MATTERS

It may be hard to know the difference between a typical age-related change and the first sign of Alzheimer's disease. To help, the Alzheimer's Association has created this list of warning signs for Alzheimer's disease and related dementias. Individuals may experience one or more of these in different degrees. If you notice any of the signs in yourself or someone you know, please see a doctor.

1. **Memory changes that disrupt daily life**
2. **Challenges in planning or solving problems**
3. **Difficulty completing familiar tasks**
4. **Confusion with time or place**
5. **Trouble understanding visual images and spatial relationships**
6. **New problems with words in speaking or writing**
7. **Misplacing things and losing the ability to retrace steps**
8. **Decreased or poor judgment**
9. **Withdrawal from work or social activities**
10. **Changes in mood and personality**

For more information about the 10 warning signs, please contact the Alzheimer's Association at **877-IS IT ALZ (877.474.8259)** or visit **www.alz.org/10signs**.

the challenge your brain
PUZZLE BOOK

level 1

KICK START YOUR NEURONS!

Mentally stimulating activities strengthen
brain cells and the connections between
them, and may even create new nerve cells.

Puzzle 1

WORDPLAY

Below are the names of six states with their vowels removed. How fast can you figure out their full names?

1. KLHM
2. NDN
3. H   _Hawaii_
4. LLNS
5. W   _Wisconsin_
6. RGN

Puzzle 2

WORDPLAY

The six words below share an unusual characteristic that's not found in many English words. What is it?

HINT: Look at these words from a different perspective.

animal
deliver
looter
diaper
drawer
straw

Puzzle 3

WORDPLAY

Below are 16 letters that form a common, everyday word. Using each given letter just once, can you figure out what the word is?

T	S	R	O
I	G	D	N
T	E	S	S
H	H	E	S

Puzzle 4
CREATIVE THINKING

CROWD

Find the hidden word or phrase!

Puzzle 5

VISUALIZATION

How many cubes are missing from the following stack that was originally 5 × 5 × 5? All rows and columns run to completion unless you actually see them end.

the **challenge** your **brain**

BONUS PUZZLE

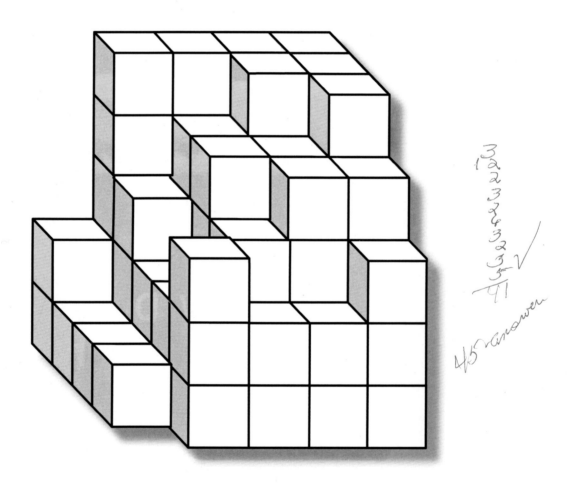

Puzzle 6
LOGIC

You are a prisoner sentenced to death. The Emperor offers you a chance to live by playing a simple game. He gives you 50 black marbles, 50 white marbles and 2 empty bowls. He then says, "Divide these 100 marbles into these 2 bowls. You can divide them any way you like as long as you use all the marbles. Then, I will blindfold you and mix the bowls around. You then can choose one bowl and remove ONE marble. If the marble is WHITE you will live, but if the marble is BLACK...you will die."

How do you divide the marbles up so that you have the greatest probability of choosing a WHITE marble?

Puzzle 7
LANGUAGE

The words below share an interesting feature that is common, basic and known to all. What is it?

HINT: Sound?

abuse
contest
permit
produce
rebel
use
convert

Puzzle 8
WORDPLAY

Five of the six words below share a characteristic not present in the sixth word. Which word is the odd one out?

HINT: Look closely

physiography
ingratiating
entertainment
underground
hotshot
tenement

Puzzle 9
WORDPLAY

You will find out this paragraph is unusual. Why? You'll find out soon, if you don't know by now. Think about what's right in front of you. Don't rush—you can sit for days or months to think about this. But, I know you won't drag this out for too long. You won't fail. I know you. Your brain will finally find a solution. By now, you probably know what's wrong with this paragraph, right? What do you think? I await your solution. I'll wait as long as you want to wait. So, what's your logical mind say about this paragraph? I know you know by now.

Puzzle 10
KNOWLEDGE

All but one of these states has a panhandle. Which is the odd one out?

Alaska
Colorado
Florida
Idaho
Oklahoma
Texas

Puzzle 11
WORDPLAY

Below is a puzzle I call a Trickledown™ puzzle. These types of puzzles were made famous by Lewis Carroll and have different names—from doublets to word ladders. Regardless of what they're called, they're fun.

In my version, you are to change one letter per word, starting with the second word. When you change a letter, the resulting word must be a word found in the dictionary. You keep changing one letter, per line until you reach the final word. Here's an example:

Example:

FULL

_____

_____

_____

PINE

Answer:

FULL

FILL

PILL

PILE

PINE

Try your skill with these:

BORN	DINGY	SENSOR
_____	_____	_____
_____	_____	_____
_____	_____	_____
CAPE	_____	_____
	PALES	_____
		TASTED

Puzzle 12

CREATIVE THINKING

Find the hidden word or phrase!

Puzzle 13
WORDPLAY

Below is a scrambled 15 letter word known to all. It begins with "S" and ends with "S". See how long it takes you to come up with this simple, straightforward word.

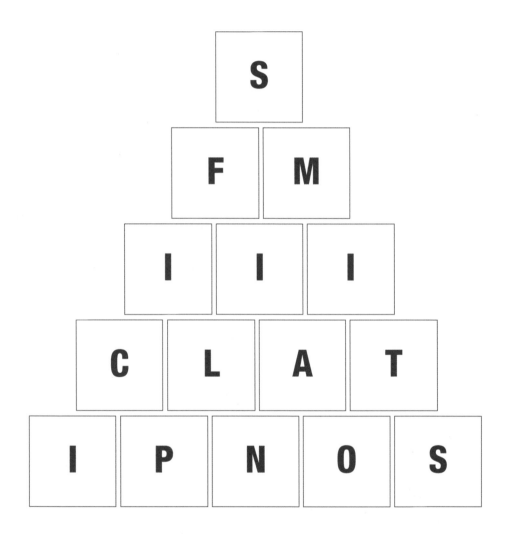

answer: _____

Puzzle 14
LOGIC

Mike's father-in-law has one daughter only. The daughter's mother-in-law has a son named Robert who has a son named Tyler. Tyler is Mike's:

A)   cousin   B)   nephew   C)   uncle

D)   son   E)   father

Puzzle 15
WORDPLAY

Unscramble the words in the column at the right to form the names of common animals. Fill in the properly spelled animal names in the space in the left column. The first letters of the correctly solved animal names, reading down, spell out the name of another animal.

					AMLEC
___	___	___	___	___	
___ ___ ___ ___ ___ ___					STORERO
___ ___ ___ ___ ___					TEROT
___ ___ ___					ACT
___ ___ ___ ___ ___ ___ ___					CHORITS
___ ___ ___ ___ ___ ___					LOPHIND
___ ___ ___ ___ ___ ___					SENICT
___ ___ ___ ___					INOL
___ ___ ___ ___ ___ ___ ___ ___					PHENTALE

Puzzle 16
MATHEMATICS

How many days are in 5,000,000 seconds?

Puzzle 17
KNOWLEDGE

Many surnames originated from people's occupations. The name Cooper came from the job of making or repairing barrels, casks and tubs. A Drover was a person who drove cattle and sheep to market. A Porter was a doorkeeper.

Match the names on the left with their respective occupations on the right.

1)	Turner	a)	Cleaner of cloth goods
2)	Lardner	b)	Forest warden
3)	Wainwright	c)	Lathe worker
4)	Woodward	d)	Keeper of fences
5)	Tucker	e)	Keeper of the cupboard
6)	Hayward	f)	One who made bows and arrows
7)	Fletcher	g)	Wagon maker

Puzzle 18
CREATIVE THINKING

Find the hidden word or phrase!

Puzzle 19
WORDPLAY

Below are three words that have more than one anagram each. See how many you can find.

earring
tacos
user

Puzzle 20
KNOWLEDGE

Fifth, fourth, third, second, first,

_____?

A) zero
B) zeroed
C) zeroth
D) zerost

Puzzle 21
WORDPLAY

Below is a common word used in everyday language. See how long it takes you to unscramble it. Some people can solve this unbelievably quickly.

ybevalnuilbe

Puzzle 22
LANGUAGE

One of the following five words does not fit with the others. Which word is it? *HINT: It has to do with the words' meanings.*

Magnanimity
Penury
Profusion
Largesse
Munificence

Puzzle 23
CREATIVE THINKING

I saw this curious note one day and had no idea what it meant.

"My very educated mother just served us nine pizzas."

When I asked a passing science professor what it meant, he smiled and said, "Oh, that slogan is being changed as we speak. It will now read,

'My very educated mother just served us nachos (no potatoes).'"

He left in a hurry and I still had no idea what it meant, but I did find out later the professor I met briefly was an astronomer.

Can you help me out and solve this riddle for me? By the way, this happened in 2006.

Puzzle 24
LOGIC

How creative are you? Can you solve for the missing letter in the last triangle and solve the triangle word game below? There is a certain logic in and around the triangles that will point you to the right answer.

Puzzle 25
LANGUAGE

One of these words is misspelled. Which one?
A)   sedulous
B)   repoire
C)   napery
D)   grommet

Puzzle 26
WORDPLAY

There is something unusual about this sentence. What is it?

"Doc note: I dissent. A fast never prevents a fatness. I diet on cod."

Puzzle 27
MATHEMATICS

Ten former classmates meet for dinner and each shakes hands with the others one time. How many total handshakes will take place among the 10 friends?

A)   100
B)   50
C)   45
D)   23
E)   11

Puzzle 28
KNOWLEDGE

One of these four sided figures, known as quadrilaterals, is different from the rest for a simple, straightforward reason. Which is the odd one out?

parallelogram   rhombus   trapezoid   square   rectangle

Puzzle 29
KNOWLEDGE

If I were to ask you on which side of the sink you'd find the cold water, I'll bet you'd have to think a few seconds before you gave me an answer.... or maybe longer. Try your luck with the following similar teasers...things we've seen a million times...but we're just not quite sure...

1. Sleepy, Happy, Sneezy, Grumpy, Dopey, Doc, and the seventh dwarf is?
2. Do books have their even-numbered pages on the left or right?
3. Name the five colors on a Campbell soup label.
4. There are two one-eyed Jacks in a typical deck of cards. Which suit faces right?
5. How many hot dog buns are in a standard package?

Puzzle 30
LANGUAGE

Here is a scrambled quote from one of America's best and funniest, Johnny Carson. See how long it takes you to unscramble this gem.

"Nothing I do as sneak barn was the so a naive I to used kid behind and."
— Johnny Carson

Puzzle 31
CREATIVE THINKING

Hsilgne

Find the hidden word or phrase!

Puzzle 32

LANGUAGE

```
E I B D O P C T H G I E W R E
E O Z E E S H R I M P F K I F
E G C R C S I C H I C K E N S
A E K C A N S C C C E L E A O
C T F P R H N E G Y B I G O P
C A P F R R R R R A T M O P E
T L R E O N H E T T U E G E A
E O R C T C C E E C N T V A P
C C P E N O G H A R L A K P S
R O T A R E G I R F E R S N K
P H O G V A R R H C Z I F T A
O C S K P A C K E M A R N R P
A R I S I R P R A I H S V T C
S A L M O N I O N S G Y R S C
T C P V L N G C E W A C E T A
```

Match the words below with the word search puzzle to the left.

recipe

milk

refrigerator

salmon

popcorn

carrot

snack

weight

cooking

grocery

chocolate

vegetable

chicken

shrimp

hazelnut

coffee

dessert

apple

spaghetti

onion

Puzzle 33

CREATIVE THINKING

Find the hidden word or phrase!

Puzzle 34
MATHEMATICS

Debbie walks by a dish where she throws her loose change. She knows there are three coins in the dish and those three coins are either dimes or nickels but she can't see them. She also knows that there is an equal chance they could be any combination of the two coins. In other words, no one has done anything to prejudice the probabilities. Her dad walks by and she tells him she'll buy him a dinner if he can tell her what the chances are that at least one dime is in the dish. He answers ¾. No dinner for Debbie's dad. Can you tell Debbie what the correct answer is?

Puzzle 35
LOGIC

You have been selected for a game show because of your keen mind. You can solve almost any logic problem. You can win $100,000 if you can solve a logic puzzle in 30 seconds with no help. You will be given four clues, three of which are false. Are you ready?

Pete: Kevin or Rachel has the check for $100,000 hidden in a shoe.
Kevin: Pete or Martha has the $100,000 check hidden in a shoe.
Martha: I don't have it.
Rachel: I have it.

Who has it?

Puzzle 36
LOGIC

Nine identical sheets of paper are used to create the design below.
If "D" were placed first, "F" placed 7th and "I" placed 9th, what order
would "B" be placed in?

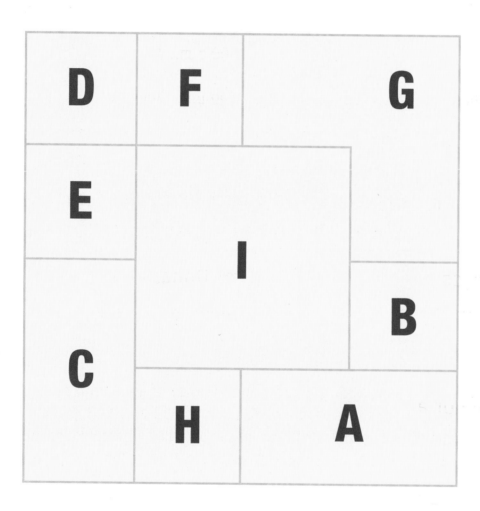

Puzzle 37
KNOWLEDGE

Which of the following countries is closest to the International Date Line?

Japan
New Zealand
New Guinea
The Netherlands
Sri Lanka

Puzzle 38
KNOWLEDGE

If it is 8:00 p.m. on a November Tuesday in Rochester, New York, what time is it in Darby, England?

8:00 p.m., Wednesday
1:00 a.m., Tuesday
1:00 a.m., Wednesday
1:00 p.m., Tuesday
12:00 p.m., Thursday

Puzzle 39
KNOWLEDGE

Here is some interesting trivia for things you see all the time but may not know their official names.

1) The name for the dots on dice?
2) The dot above the "i"?
3) The pound sign #?
4) The attachment of the top of a lamp that usually screws into the lamp to hold the shade in place?
5) The plastic tip of a shoelace?

Puzzle 40
CREATIVE THINKING

M

I

GHT

Find the hidden word or phrase!

Puzzle 41
CREATIVE THINKING

Here's a new type of tic-tac-toe. We'll call it cit-cat-cot, because in this version, three in a row loses! Below is the start of a game and it's X's turn to move.

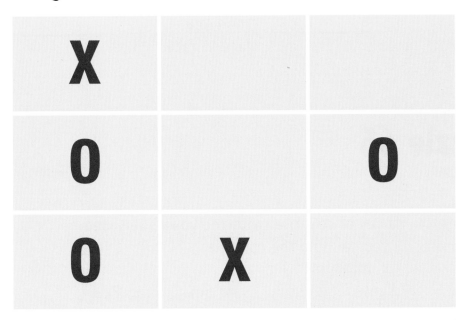

Where is the best square to place your X?

Puzzle 42
MATHEMATICS

Two fathers and three sons found six coins on a walk. They split the coins evenly among them. How was this possible?

Puzzle 43
KNOWLEDGE

Besides Kentucky and Virginia, what are the states adjacent to West Virginia?

Puzzle 44
WORDPLAY

Match these abbreviations with their respective meanings on the right.

1)	i.e.	a)	for example
2)	e.g.	b)	the same place
3)	vis-a-vis	c)	that is
4)	ibid	d)	therefore
5)	ergo	e)	face to face

Puzzle 45
WORDPLAY

Below are the names of countries with the vowels removed.
See how quickly you can find the countries.

1) Thlnd   2) Rgntn   3) Strl   4) Srnm   5) Pkstn

Puzzle 46
MATHEMATICS

30 heads plus 100 feet
Both bucks and ducks are there to meet.
But is there a way to count these things?
The thought of it spins my head in rings.

So, tell me my friends, if you think you can
The number of each animal in this band.

Puzzle 47

Believe it or not, only one number is spelled with all of its letters in alphabetical order in the English language...and only one number has all of its letters in reverse alphabetical order. See how long it takes you to come up with both numbers. Better yet, once you know the answers, try this puzzle at a party or gathering of people. You may be surprised how much fun this can generate.

Puzzle 48

A group of journalism graduate students were asked to write down what newspapers they read from a large city. 69% were reading the *Sun-Times*, 21% were reading the *Tribune* and 12% were reading both. What percentage of the students were not reading any newspaper?

Puzzle 49
WORDPLAY

Here's an example of a word puzzle called the "Front end add on" puzzle. It works like this: Pick a three-, four- or five-letter word to add on to the front of another word so that the end result creates a brand new word.

Example:

___ ___ ___ roll   ___ ___ ___ ___ frame   ___ ___ ___ ___ ___ clean

___ ___ ___ master   ___ ___ ___ ___ stay   ___ ___ ___ ___ ___ boat

___ ___ ___ able   ___ ___ ___ ___ sail   ___ ___ ___ ___ ___ broken

Answers:

p **a** **y** roll   **m** **a** **i** **n** frame   **h** **o** **u** **s** **e** clean

p **a** **y** master   **m** **a** **i** **n** stay   **h** **o** **u** **s** **e** boat

p **a** **y** able   **m** **a** **i** **n** sail   **h** **o** **u** **s** **e** broken

Now, try these:

___ ___ ___ pole   ___ ___ ___ ___ loose   ___ ___ ___ ___ ___ power

___ ___ ___ flower   ___ ___ ___ ___ hills   ___ ___ ___ ___ ___ laugh

___ ___ ___ hem   ___ ___ ___ ___ bridge   ___ ___ ___ ___ ___ whip

Puzzle 50
WORDPLAY

There are supposed to be more than 25 parts of the body which are spelled with four letters. Don't worry about being too technical. It's strictly for fun, so anything goes.

Example: Iris, Nose, Lung, Neck, Knee, Face, etc.

How many can you find?

Puzzle 51

CREATIVE THINKING

A spy needs to get a secret document to Rome and the only way he can travel is by train. The security at the depot has been tipped off to be on the lookout for people trying to board trains with items over four feet long. They are measuring all carry-on luggage that looks close. The dilemma: the spy has been transporting 5-foot-long maps and needs to deliver another one by tomorrow morning. He can't hide it in his clothing, nor fold it in half, and his attaché is exactly four feet long by three and a half feet wide. Can you help to get him and his map on the train?

Puzzle 52

LOGIC

Below is a letter square with the letter Q missing so as to make a 5 × 5 square. Now, here's the puzzle: Find the letter that comes just above the letter that comes between the letter just before the letter just below G and the letter just before the letter just above T.

A	B	C	D	E
F	G	H	I	J
K	L	M	N	O
P	R	S	T	U
V	W	X	Y	Z

Puzzle 53

CREATIVE THINKING

C R O W D
      U
      T

Find the hidden word or phrase!

Puzzle 54
LANGUAGE

Put this sentence back into everyday English:

It is highly inadvisable and certainly a waste of time and possibly money, to use a calculator or other device, including fingers to enumerate a certain, well-known worldwide avian species while those to be tallied are not yet in existence.

Puzzle 55
LOGIC

What number comes first in the sequence below?

?   1   8   6   13   11   18   16   23   21   28

Puzzle 56
CREATIVE THINKING

Mrs. Periwinkle left on a trip the day after the day before yesterday and she will be back the eve of the day after tomorrow. How many days is she away?

his years   yyyyyyy

Find the hidden word or phrase!

Puzzle 58

CREATIVE THINKING

DUMB   DUMB

WORD   WORD

WORD   WORD

Find the hidden word or phrase!

Puzzle 59
LANGUAGE

Which of the following words is misspelled?

1) connoisseur
2) sergeant
3) necessarily
4) repertoire
5) supercillious
6) cemetery

Puzzle 60
MATHEMATICS

Two-thirds of a pound of cheese is balanced perfectly by one-third of a block of the same cheese. What is the weight of the whole block of cheese?

Puzzle 61
MATHEMATICS

If you have a full glass of water, pour out half, then pour back in half of what you poured out, pour out a third of what you now have and pour back in a third of a glass, what fraction of the glass is full?

Puzzle 62

KNOWLEDGE

Below are some symbols on the left that you see every day. Match the symbol with its respective meaning on the right. These symbols are usually found either over, between or in front of letters and words.

1. ^   A. Umlaut
2. ¨   B. Tilde
3. #   C. Ampersand
4. ~   D. Caret
5. &   E. Octothorpe or Pound
6. /   F. Virgule

Puzzle 63

LOGIC

Imagine you have two identical floor fans that both rotate clockwise. Have them face each other and turn one of the fans on. The air should be blowing directly into the other fan, which is turned off. What will happen to the movement of the blades of the fan that is turned off?

1) The blades move clockwise.
2) The blades move counterclockwise.
3) The blades remain stationary.
4) The blades start clockwise, then rotate counterclockwise, then clockwise, ... back and forth.

Puzzle 64

VIUAL

How many squares of any size are in the picture below?

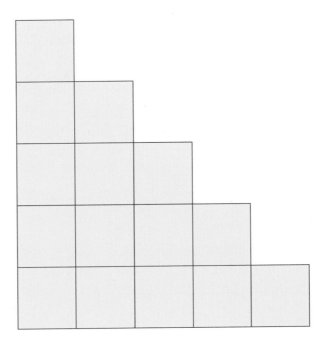

Puzzle 65

VISUAL

What is the total number of individual cubes below? All rows and columns run to completion unless you actually see them end.

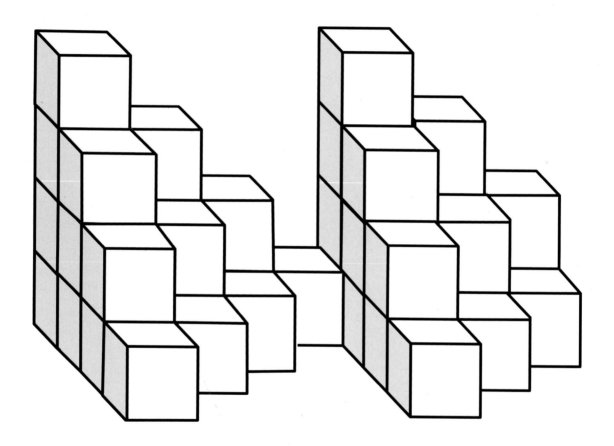

Puzzle 66
LOGIC

Bob McGuire met an old friend and teammate from high school. After catching up on their lives, the friend said to Bob, "I married someone you never knew and this is our daughter," showing her picture. The friend continued, "She has the same name as her mother." Bob quickly responded, "Molly is a good, strong name." How did Bob know his friend's daughter's name?

Puzzle 67
LANGUAGE

What is the smallest natural number that contains all six vowels

a, e, i, o, u, and y?

Puzzle 68
MATHEMATICS

Here is an interesting math puzzle that is not as difficult as it appears. Can you find a number that when divided by 2, has a remainder of 1; when divided by 3, has a remainder of 2; when divided by 4, has a remainder of 3; when divided by 5, has a remainder of 4; and when divided by 6, has a remainder of 5? Lowest number please.

Puzzle 69
CREATIVE THINKING

Find the hidden word or phrase!

the challenge your brain
PUZZLE BOOK

level 2

FIRE UP YOUR SYNAPSES!

Solve these puzzles with a friend or family member. Social activity not only makes physical and mental activity more enjoyable, it can reduce stress levels, which helps maintain healthy connections among brain cells.

Puzzle 70

LOGIC

You are playing a game with 12 matchsticks, in which two players take turns removing from 1 to 3 matchsticks on each turn. The winner is the player who picks up the last matchstick.

Your friend goes first and picks up 1 matchstick. Is there a definite number you can pick up to assure your victory on your first move?

Puzzle 71

LOGIC

Alphametics are fun because they spell out a phrase, slogan, person's name, movie, etc. For the uninitiated, alphametics (also called cryptarithms) are number/letter puzzles where letters represent digits in an addition problem. Here's an example:

```
   SOLVE           41652
       A               9
+ LITTLE        + 687762
--------        --------
 TEASER          729423
```

Here's an updated version.
It has 2 solutions.
O = 0
A = 9
S = 8
for both solutions.

```
   SOLVE           _ _ _ _ _
       A                   _
+ LARGE         + _ _ _ _ _
--------        ---------
 TEASER          _ _ _ _ _ _
```

Puzzle 72
LOGIC

Four of the five shapes below can be created without lifting the pencil, retracing, backtracking or crossing any lines. Which one cannot?

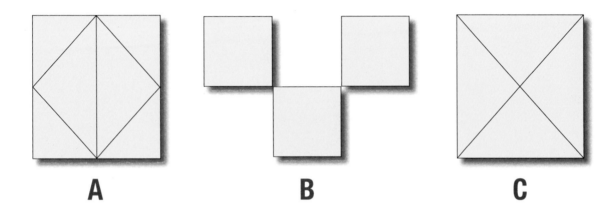

A   **B**   **C**

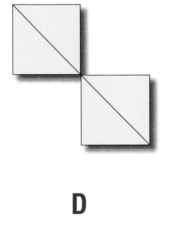   

D   **E**

Puzzle 73
CREATIVE THINKING

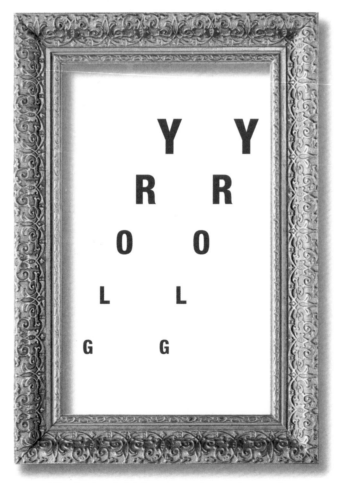

Find the hidden word or phrase!

Puzzle 74
LOGIC

Place 6 different cards in a row on a table. The third card from the left is a Queen of Diamonds. How many different arrangements of the six cards are possible if the Queen of Diamonds can never be at either end of the row?

Puzzle 75
KNOWLEDGE

Try your skill at these following units of time:

1) A Microsecond is what fraction of a second?
2) A Lustrum is how many years?
3) A sesquicentennial is how many years?
4) Ephemeral is how long (by definition)?
5) Can you put these in order from longest time period to shortest?
   epoch, era, period, eon

Puzzle 76
LOGIC

My uncle is three times as old as my sister, who is twice as old as my brother, who is twice as old as our cousin. The total of all our ages is divisible by five and less than 100. How old is my cousin?

Puzzle 77

LOGIC

Below is a rectangle that is 79 × 74. There are 3 squares marked A, B, and C under the 10" square. What are the dimensions of each square knowing that every figure contained within the entire frame is a square? (NOTE: There is a very small square just above the upper right-hand corner of C whose size is not marked.)

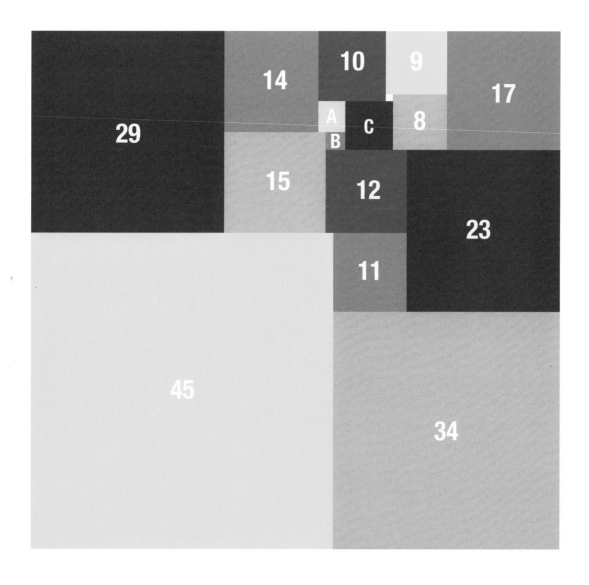

Puzzle 78
KNOWLEDGE

You might know that Denver is called the Mile High City and Boston is known as Beantown. See if you can match up these international cities with their nicknames.

1. Athens of the North	a. Lima
2. City of the Kings	b. Rome
3. Queen of the Mediterranean	c. Prague
4. The Eternal City	d. Venice
5. City of a Thousand Spires	e. Edinburgh

Puzzle 79
KNOWLEDGE

Here are some analogies that will test even the best players:

1) Steel : iron :: coke : _____

2) Japan : sun :: _____ : Southern Cross

3) Equinox : March :: Winter Solstice: _____

4) Hephaestus: Greek :: _____ : Roman

Puzzle 80
WORDPLAY

Ciphers and codes offer some of the best challenges and fun in puzzleland. Here are 4 humorous cryptograms for you to uncode. I'm sure you'll like the humor once you solve them.

a) RFYLIQ RM KMBCPL KCBGAYJ YBTLACQ QSAF YQ
YLRGZGMRGAQ, LYQYJ QNPYW, YLB BGCR AMIC, GR FYQ
ZCAMKC PMSRGLC DMP NCMNJC GL RFC AGTGJGXCB
UMPJB RM NYQQ RFC YEC MD DMPRW, QMKCRGKCQ KMPC
RFLY MLAC. —MYTC ZYPPW

b) CO Y PYO'R PCEEHK TKYIR SBKIK CR RVYIVKHT Y ZYIS QF
SBK DQET BK JQWHE BKRCSYSK SQ SWIO QNKI SQ SBK
ZIQZKI YWSBQICSCKR. —K.D. JBCSK

c) HMEKZSHNM HR VGDM XNT OZX EHESDDM CNKKZQR ENQ
SGD SDM-CNKKZQ GZHQBTS XNT TRDC SN FDS ENQ EHUD
CNKKZQR VGDM XNT GZC GZHQ. −RZL DVHMF

d) CQGH A CXZ LENHSGB, A DENYM BGIGITGB XHLVQAHS,
CQGVQGB AV QXM QXUUGHGM EB HEV; TNV IL
KXDNYVAGZ XBG MGDXLAHS HEC XHM ZEEH A ZQXYY
TG ZE A DXHHEV BGIGITGB XHL TNV VQG VQAHSZ VQXV
HGOGB QXUUGHGM. AV AZ ZXM VE SE VE UAGDGZ YARG
VQAZ TNV CG XYY QXOG VE ME AV. −IXBR VCXAH

Puzzle 81
KNOWLEDGE

Analogies:

1) Moby Dick : Melville : : The Last of the Mohicans : _____
2) Joe Montana : S.F. 49'ers : : Sid Luckman : _____
3) Mona Lisa : DaVinci : : The Scream : _____
4) Yesterday: Beatles : : White Rabbit : _____
5) 6 : Insect : : 8 : _____
6) Obama : Biden : : Carter : _____
7) Heart : Cardiology : : Hypothalamus : _____
8) Goddess of Love (Greek) : Aphrodite : : Goddess of Love (Roman) : _____
9) Above : supra- : : Beneath : _____
10) Fear of being alone : Monophobia : : Fear of being in crowds : _____
11) FBI : Acronyms : : to, two, too : _____

Puzzle 82
KNOWLEDGE

Match the legal terms in the left column with their respective meaning in the right column.

1) voir dire
2) exculpatory
3) amicus curiae
4) corpus delecti
5) judicial notice

a) a person, not a party to the case, who offers information to the court to assist in the decision
b) a crime must be proven to have been committed before anyone can be tried
c) prospective jurors are questioned by counsel
d) a rule in which the court takes notice of facts that are known with certainty to be true
e) a type of evidence that tends to clear or excuse a defendant from fault

Puzzle 83
CREATIVE THINKING

FRAME™ GAME
Just for Fun!

Find the hidden word or phrase!

Puzzle 84
KNOWLEDGE

One of these famous scientists never won the Nobel Prize in physics. Who is the odd one out?

Richard Feynman
Albert Einstein
Murray Gell-Mann
Niels Bohr
Marie Curie
Stephen Hawking

Puzzle 85
MATHEMATICS

I am thinking of a fraction where 5/9 is 11/13 of that fraction. What is it?

Puzzle 86
KNOWLEDGE

We often see Latin phrases used in literature, newspapers, magazines, and even billboards. They're fun to try and figure out. Phrases such as "carpe diem" – seize the day and "tempus fugit" – time flies, are used all the time. On the left are some Latin phrases that are still seen today. Match them to their respective meaning in the right-hand column.

1) ipso facto
2) anguis in herba
3) alea iacta est
4) cogito ergo sum
5) ex nihilo nihil fit
6) viam inveniam aut faciam

a) I think, therefore I am
b) I will find a way or make one
c) The die has been cast
d) By the fact itself
e) Nothing comes from nothing
f) snake in the grass

Puzzle 87
MATHEMATICS

What two fractions come next?

1/3   4/5   2/4   5/6   3/5   6/7   4/6   7/8   ☐ ☐

Puzzle 88
WORDPLAY

The following is a well-known saying expressed in an unusual way. See how long it takes you to decipher this well-known phrase.

"It is a fact of Newtonian physics that a conglomerate with mass M, sometimes with a constant velocity but most often accelerating, will not have the capacity at any point T in time, to attach itself to any bryophyte."

Puzzle 89
LOGIC

Each of the four-sided figures in the grid below is a square.

1) How big is the smallest square (orange)?
2) What is the size of square "A" (purple)?

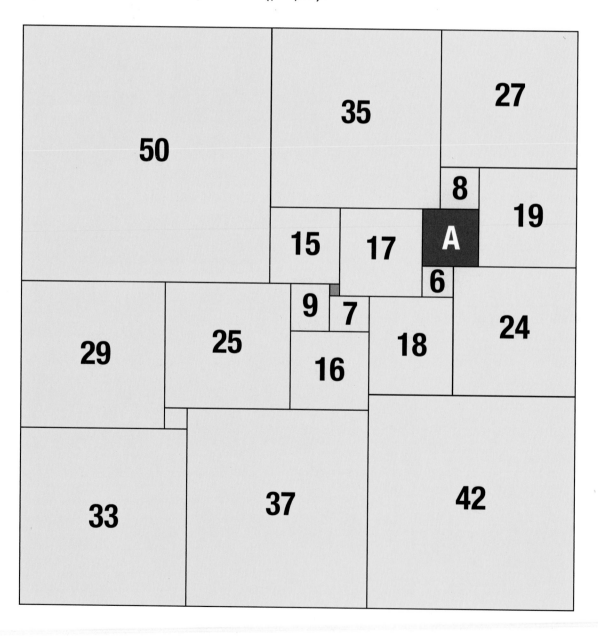

Puzzle 90
WORDPLAY

Below are several phrases that are anagrams of the names of well-known people, both living and deceased. See how quickly you can come up with their names.

A) Me, radium ace (scientist)
B) I'll make a wise phrase (playwright)
C) Bursting presence (American Rock 'N Roller)
D) Old West Action (actor/director)
E) Edge? Ref error (tennis great) (the question mark is not part of anagram)

Puzzle 91
MATHEMATICS

Try this baseball math:

The distance from home plate to the pitcher's mound is 60 feet, 6 inches. A 90 mph fastball will reach the plate in 0.458 seconds.

If you moved back 90 feet from home plate, how many feet per second would the ball have to travel to reach the plate in 0.458 seconds?

Puzzle 92
LOGIC

You and a friend decide to go see a Minnesota Twins baseball game. Your friend says he is willing to toss a coin to see who purchases the tickets. He says that he is going to toss the coin three times and if heads comes up 2 out of those 3 tosses, he will buy both tickets. Are you getting the better end of the deal?

Puzzle 93
WORDPLAY

The following sentences have two blanks that can be filled with two words that are anagrams of each other. Here's an example:

The building was of __RECENT__ construction, but the cement had been of poor quality and the __CENTER__ was crumbling.

Now try these:

1. The coach did not mind being the _____. His last place team knew how to handle the constant pressure of the fans and media. Team members had class, character and were well _____ in who they were and what was important.

2. The entire coalition of the country's _____ rallied together and chanted their demands in _____ so the nation would sympathize with their deplorable working conditions.

3. After 20 years of service, the conductor finally had enough seniority to hold a job starting out of his home _____. It was called the "old _____" route because it followed the exact route of the old streetcars.

Puzzle 94
WORDPLAY

As far as I know, this type of puzzle has no specific name. They've been around for over 50 years and are great fun to solve. Here's how they look.

Example:
1) 26 L of the A
2) 9 I in a B G
3) 8 P of S in the E L

Your job is to come up with the common phrase, idiom, book, song title, game, etc.

The answers:
1) 26 Letters of the Alphabet
2) 9 Innings in a Baseball Game
3) 8 Parts of Speech in the English Language

Here are 30 more for you to decipher:

1) 7 W. of the A. W.
2) 1001 A. N.
3) 12 S. of the Z.
4) 54 C. in a D. (with J.)
5) 9 P. in the S. S.
6) 88 P. K.
7) 13 S. on the A. F.
8) 32 D. F. at which W. F.
9) 1 D. at a T.
10) 18 H. on a G. C.
11) 90 D. in a R. A.
12) 50 C. in a H. D.
13) 8 S. on a S. S.
14) 3 B. M. (S. H. T. R.)
15) 4 Q. in a G.
16) 24 H. in a D.
17) 1 W. on a U.
18) 5 D. in a Z. C.
19) 57 H. V.
20) 11 P. on a F. T.
21) 7 H. of R.
22) 101 D.
23) 64 S. on a C. B.
24) 13 C. in a S.
25) 10 L. I.
26) 20,000 L. U. T. S.
27) 13 O. C.
28) 12 K. of the R. T.
29) 13 in a B. D.
30) 66 B. of the B.

Puzzle 95

LANGUAGE

Anything is fair game as far as puzzle material goes. Below are some of the best-known gods and goddesses in Greek mythology. Can you come up with their Roman counterparts? (Example: The Greek god Zeus is known as Jupiter in Roman mythology.)

1. Poseidon
2. Hera
3. Ares
4. Athena
5. Hermes
6. Artemis

Puzzle 96

VISUAL

Four of the five figures below can be drawn with one continuous movement of a pen or pencil, without crossing any lines, retracing or lifting of the pen or pencil to perform any trickery or other movement. One of the drawings is impossible to create without crossing lines or retracing. Which is the odd one out?

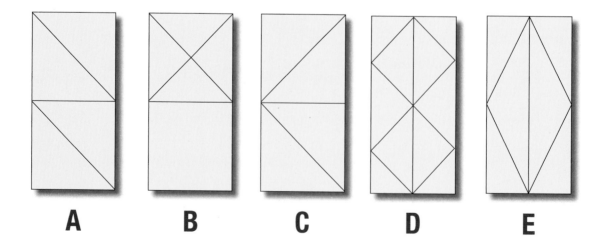

A   B   C   D   E

Puzzle 97
WORDPLAY

This puzzle is called a "squeezer" because a word has to be "squeezed" between two other words to create two new words. Here's an example:

Bath ___ ___ ___ ___ ___ boat   Bath **h** **o** **u** **s** **e** boat

bathhouse and **houseboat**

In each squeezer, the number of dashes between the two given words represents the number of letters in that word.

1) World ___ ___ ___ ___ spread   4) Brain ___ ___ ___ ___ ___ birth
2) Place ___ ___ ___ ___ stand   5) Sweet ___ ___ ___ ___ ___ strings
3) Hard ___ ___ ___ ___ house   6) Light ___ ___ ___ ___ ___ read

Puzzle 98
LANGUAGE

You may know that dogs are often referred to as canines, cows as bovines, and cats as felines...but almost all animals have similar type adjectives to describe them. See if you can match the animals on the left with their respective animal adjective on the right.

1) fox   a) delphine
2) moose   b) leporine
3) rabbit   c) lupine
4) wolf   d) vulpine
5) dolphin   e) ovine
6) leopard   f) pardine
7) sheep   g) cervine

Puzzle 99
MATHEMATICS

Mindy and Mandy each want to buy their favorite candy bar at a store on the way home from school. One girl is 58 cents short and the other is 25 cents short. When they combine their money, they still don't have enough to buy one candy bar. What is the most one candy bar could cost?

Puzzle 100
LOGIC

Alex's father-in-law's only son's mother-in-law's daughter could be Alex's:

a. mom
b. grandmother
c. sister-in-law
d. cousin
e. daughter
f. niece

Puzzle 101
VISUAL

Below are 4 squares made with matchsticks. Move 2 and only 2 of the matchsticks to create 5 squares.

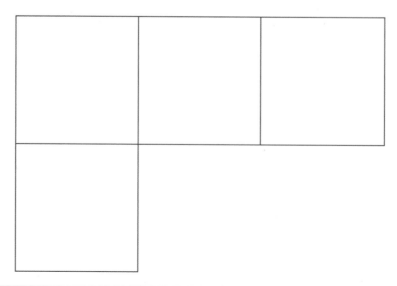

Puzzle 102
MATHEMATICS

In a 9-inning game, what is the minimum number of pitches that a pitcher, who pitches the whole game, can throw?

Hint: Remember, there are at least two pitchers in every game.

Puzzle 103
MATHEMATICS

At a reception, 1/6 of the guests departed at a certain time. Later, 2/5 of the remaining guests departed. Even later, 3/4 of those guests departed. If 15 people were left, how many were originally at the party?

Puzzle 104
LOGIC

John monitors 3 different machines during his shift at work. Each has a different probability of breaking down during a shift.

Machine #1: 4/7
Machine #2: 2/13
Machine #3: 3/11

What is the probability that none of the machines will break down during a shift?

Puzzle 105
CREATIVE THINKING

MUSIC 11 EARS

Find the hidden word or phrase!

Puzzle 106
MATHEMATICS

If 1/2 of 9 were 6, what would 1/6 of 12 be?

Puzzle 107
MATHEMATICS

A number can be divided into 1,150 and 1,254 and have the same remainder. What is the smallest three-digit number greater than 100 that makes this true?

Puzzle 108
KNOWLEDGE

If it takes three minutes to boil an egg to your taste at sea level, will it take a longer or shorter time for the egg to cook to your taste at a 10,000 foot elevation?

Puzzle 109
LOGIC

One of five brothers ate a plate of cookies his mother had made for a party. All the brothers denied eating the cookies, but each made two statements about who did eat the cookies. In each case, one of the statements was true; one was false.

After their mom heard the boys' statements, she knew immediately who the culprit was. See how long it takes you to find the guilty brother.

Bart: It wasn't Bruno.
It was Bret.

Bret: It wasn't Brit.
It wasn't Bruno.

Brit: It was Bruno.
It wasn't Bart.

Boone: It was Brit.
It was Bret.

Bruno: It was Boone.
It wasn't Bart.

Puzzle 110
MATHEMATICS

You have a five-minute timer and a three-minute timer. They are both of the hourglass variety where sand filtering from one chamber to another marks the time. How would you accurately mark the passing of seven minutes?

Puzzle 111
KNOWLEDGE

All of the following tennis greats won Grand Slam titles in tennis. The French Open eluded all but one of the following players. This player not only won the French Open, but captured the other three Grand Slam titles, as well. Who holds all four Grand Slam tennis titles?

Jimmey Connors
John McEnroe
Pete Sampras
Andre Agassi
Stefan Edberg

Puzzle 112
LOGIC

A group of 100 football players suffered the following injuries while playing: 70 ballplayers injured their arm, 75 injured their leg, 85 injured their hand, and 80 injured their shoulder. What is the minimum number of ballplayers who must have suffered all 4 injuries?

Puzzle 113
VISUAL

Here's a new twist on the pyramid scrambled word game. Each pyramid below contains a common, everyday word. Put the two words together and you have a common two-word phrase known to all.

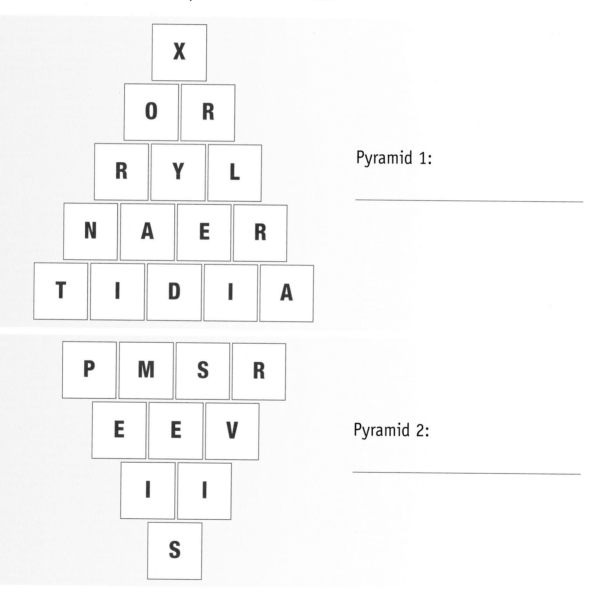

Pyramid 1:

_____

Pyramid 2:

_____

The Phrase: _____

Puzzle 114
LANGUAGE

Six of the seven words below share a common characteristic that the seventh word doesn't. Which word is the odd one out and why?

ensign	mould	half	present
stream	psychology	knives	

Puzzle 115
LOGIC

Sometimes puzzles and problems appear to lack all the necessary information. This puzzle falls into that category. Upon first glance, you would swear there is not enough information – but a closer look will reveal that there is. Give it a try and see how flexible your mind can become!

What is the value of F?

A + B = Z
Z + P = T
T + A = F
B + P + F = 130
A = 20

Puzzle 116
MATHEMATICS

If P is 3/4 of Q,
and Q is 2/3 of R,
and R is 1/2 of S,
what is the ratio of S to P?

Puzzle 117

MATHEMATICS

My present age is 6 times what it will be 6 years from now minus 6 times what it was 6 years ago. How old am I?

HINT: This is easier than it sounds. Set up a legend of what you know and what equals what.

Puzzle 118

MATHEMATICS

A 150-pound mixture of chemicals cost $40. It is composed of one type of chemical that costs $48 per 150 pounds and another type of chemical that costs $36 per 150 pounds.

How many pounds of each chemical were used in the mixture?

Puzzle 119
WORDPLAY

Below are seven "famous fill-ins." They may be a person's name, a well-known place, movie, song, etc. I'll give you a few letters and the correct number of blanks and letters in each word.

Example:

S __ __ Q __ __ __ T __ N

The answer is San Quentin.

Now try these:

1) __ U L __ __ __ __ __ E __ A __

(Historical Figure)

2) T __ __ __ __ O __ T __ __ T __ __ P A __ __ Y

(American History Incident)

3) S __ __ __ N __ __ O __ __ H __ __ __ A M __ __ __

(Movie)

4) __ __ __ N S __ __ __ __ H U __ __ __ __ __ __ L

(English Historical Figure)

5) __ E R __ __ __ W __ __ __ __ I A __ __

(Athlete)

6) P U __ __ __ __ Z E __ P __ __ __ Z __'

(Award)

7) __ __ E __ R __ __ __ __ U __ __ E __ D

(Musical Group)

Puzzle 120
WORDPLAY

```
P R T S I T N E D T G P U Z L E O E
G A M B L I N G L R U R K B D C D E P
B N I O E O D E S S E R T A O R L E A
G F O R T U N L E Z A H R N D L U Y I
K A H I P O R L G P C O O K I N G G N
P C M E T L R O O R Y M P K E C G R T
C T E E M C A C N E Y E S E G G A E R
R O B H G I E N Y S A O S R R D G N I
B R M E C N L L E C H W A T U D E E O
M Y G P E Y B L E R L N P L U K S O M
S U F H U T A E E I D E T B C N R S E
H E Y E G T T P T P P R C I A K E E M
R E F R I G E R A T O R H C I N E M A
I L N G T L G R L I P C K O I F R C R
M T I F E N E B O O C M S O F T A E E
P D P V I N V R C N O A R O O R C R M
G O A V T A A E O G R O C E R Y T R O
C R A G W E I G H T N U E O M O O O O
T S R T I D E R C P S E T H A C H R B
```

Match the words below with the word search puzzle to the left.

budget	economy	passport
chicken	drug	horoscope
computer	homeowner	boomer
gambling	credit	grocery
dentist	popcorn	prescription
career	ski	coffee
airplane	weight	paint
refrigerator	election	neighbor
adult	cooking	paycheck
travel	college	digital
snack	hazelnut	energy
puzzle	gym	benefit
senior	grandparent	carrot
vegetable	factory	park
saving	luggage	game
shrimp	bank	memoir
motorcycle	relief	chocolate
dessert	cinema	

Puzzle 121
MATHEMATICS

A publisher is printing an article of 48,000 words. Two sizes of type will be used: one where a page consists of 900 words. The other will have 1500 words on a page. The article will be 40 pages long. How many pages of each type will be used?

Puzzle 122
KNOWLEDGE

A gazelle has one.
An eagle has one.
A kangaroo has two.
A pheasant has two and a lion has none.
How many does an anaconda have?

Puzzle 123
WORDPLAY

Below is a jumbled quote from Shakespeare (Julius Caesar). See if you can unscramble the words to come up with the correct quote.

"Death times many before cowards but taste once never the die of their valiant deaths."

Puzzle 124
CREATIVE THINKING

1. Cello
2. Violin
3. Guitar
4. Ukelele
5. Bass

Find the hidden word or phrase!

Puzzle 125

VISUAL

This figure can be divided with 2 straight cuts in such a way that the resulting pieces can fit together to form a rectangle whose length is twice its width. How can this be accomplished?

Puzzle 126
WORDPLAY

Of all the puzzles I've run across, finding triple homonyms have been at the top of the list for puzzle enthusiasts everywhere. It's also in a group of puzzles I call "project puzzles:" you can take as long as you need and work on these when you find the time. In any event, they can be great fun. To warm up, here are a few—

1) cent, scent, sent
2) pair, pear, pare
3) do, doe, dough

When I compiled my list, I tried to ensure the words sounded alike as reasonably as possible. Therefore, I excluded several homonyms I had seen previously like weather, wether, whether or homonyms that included a proper noun like Chile, chili, chilly. If there are more than three that is acceptable.

But the list I created in the answer section is a guide for you to create your own list. Make it an ongoing project and add to it as time permits. I think you'll see it can be great fun.

Puzzle 127
VISUAL

Figure 1 below is a square piece of paper, Figure 2 is the piece of paper folded in half, from left to right and Figure 3 in fourths, top folded over to bottom.

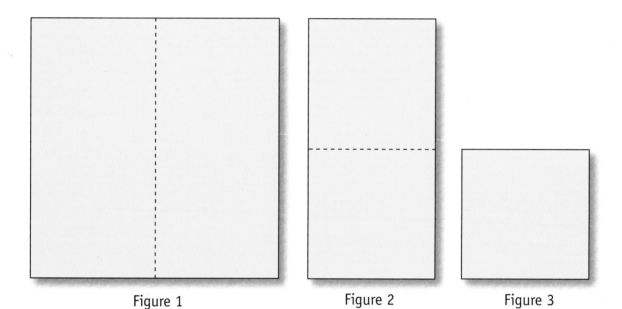

Figure 1   Figure 2   Figure 3

Now, imagine that you have snipped off the corners of Figure 3 as shown in Figure 4.

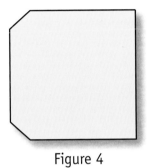

Figure 4

Now, open the piece of paper. The resulting figure will look like:

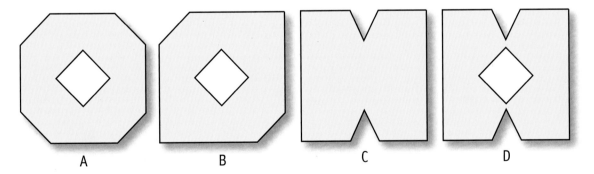

A   B   C   D

Puzzle 128

LOGIC

8 hours ago it was 6 hours before there would be ¾ of the day already gone. (The day starts at 12 a.m.) What time is it now?

Puzzle 129

KNOWLEDGE

Here's a puzzle dealing with physical geography. See if you can match the left side with the right side.

1.	Palouse	A.	A row of cliffs along the western banks of the Hudson River in New Jersey.
2.	Pampas		
3.	Piedmont	B.	Scenic, rolling hills found in Washington.
4.	Palisades	C.	Flat, fertile plains in South America.
		D.	A plateau region lying between a coastal plain and a mountain.

Puzzle 130
KNOWLEDGE

A few quick analogy puzzles...

1. Anterior : Posterior : : Dorsal : _____

2. Pronate : Palm Down : : _____ : Palm Up

3. 3 : Babe Ruth : : _____ : Lou Gehrig

4. Probability : 3 out of 8 : : Odds : _____

5. Pros : Amateurs (U.S.) : : Ryder Cup : _____

Puzzle 131
WORDPLAY

The words and phrases below are all anagrams of famous authors. Here is an example:

RACE NINE = Anne Rice

1) COWARDS LIE
2) HO! EDITORS GLEE
3) ENRAGING BULLS
4) NEWS-THEN IMAGERY
5) SEARCH SLICK END

Puzzle 132

KNOWLEDGE

Only two states in the United States can make the claim that they have eight bordering states. One of those is Missouri. What is the other state?

Puzzle 133

VISUAL

What number goes in the last box?

2	-7
20	11

12	40
-17	11

48	14
61	27

5	9
7	11

4	4
3	?

answer key

level 1

puzzle 1
1. Oklahoma
2. Indiana
3. Ohio
4. Illinois
5. Iowa
6. Oregon

puzzle 2
Each word forms a new word when read backward. This type of pairing is called a "recurrent palindrome."

puzzle 3
Shortsightedness

puzzle 4
Faces in the Crowd

puzzle 5
There are 45 cubes missing

puzzle 6
Place 1 white marble in one bowl, and place the rest of the marbles in the other bowl (49 whites, and 50 blacks).

This way you begin with a 50/50 chance of choosing the bowl with just one white marble, therefore life! BUT even if you choose the other bowl, you still have ALMOST a 50/50 chance at picking one of the 49 white marbles.

puzzle 7
Each of the words can be pronounced two different ways and has two different meanings. Each word is both a noun and a verb. Words like this are called heteronyms.

puzzle 8
Tenement is the odd one out. The other 5 words start and end with the same trigram (three-letter group) in the same order.

puzzle 9
There are no "e's" in the entire paragraph and the letter "e" is the most often used letter in the English language.

puzzle 10
Colorado does not have a panhandle.

puzzle 11
BORN	DINGY	SENSOR
BORE	DINGS	TENSOR
CORE	PINGS	TENSER
CARE	PINES	TENTER
CAPE	PANES	TENTED
	PALES	TESTED
		TASTED

puzzle 12
Downright Crazy

puzzle 13
Simplifications

puzzle 14
B) nephew

puzzle 15
CAMEL
ROOSTER
OTTER
CAT
OSTRICH
DOLPHIN
INSECT
LION
ELEPHANT
CROCODILE

puzzle 16
There are 57.87 days in 5,000,000 seconds.

puzzle 17
1-c; 2-e; 3-g; 4-b; 5-a; 6-d; 7-f

puzzle 18
Fanny Pack

puzzle 19
Earring: rearing, angrier, grainer, rangier.
Tacos: coast, ascot, coats, costa.
User: sure, suer, ruse, rues.

puzzle 20
C) zeroth

puzzle 21
Unbelievably

puzzle 22
Penury, which is stinginess or miserliness, doesn't fit with the others. All the other words have to do with generosity.

puzzle 23
These are slogans to be used as memory aids to remember the names of the planets - from closest to the sun to furthest - Mercury, Venus, Earth, Mars, Jupiter, Saturn, Uranus, Neptune, and Pluto. The first letters of each of the planets are the first letters of the words in the slogans. When it was decided by the scientific community in 2006 that Pluto would no longer be considered a planet, the second slogan came into play -- (no potatoes) meaning not Pluto.

puzzle 24
Beginning with the "C" in the first triangle and moving counter clockwise in each successive triangle, the phrase spells out "Can you solve this puzzle?" The missing letter is "E".

puzzle 25
B) repoire – it's not even a word.

puzzle 26
The sentence is palindromic. It reads the same forward and backward.

puzzle 27
C) 45   9 + 8 + 7 + 6 + 5 + 4 + 3 + 2 + 1

puzzle 28
Trapezoid is the odd one out. The others have two sets of parallel lines. A trapezoid has one set only of parallel lines.

puzzle 29
1. Bashful
2. Left
3. Red, White, Black, Gold, Silver
4. The Jack of Spades faces right
5. There are 8 hot dog buns in a standard package

puzzle 30
"I was so naive as a kid I used to sneak behind the barn and do nothing."

puzzle 31
Reverse English

puzzle 32

puzzle 33
Head for Home

puzzle 34
7/8. The possibilities: 7 of the 8 following combinations have at least one dime, as well as one nickel.

dime, dime, dime
dime, dime, nickel
dime, nickel, dime
dime, nickel, nickel

nickel, nickel, nickel
nickel, nickel, dime
nickel, dime, nickel
nickel, dime, dime

puzzle 35
Martha has the check.

puzzle 36
"B" is sixth. Here is the complete order:
D E C H A B F G I

puzzle 37
New Zealand

puzzle 38
1:00 a.m., Wednesday. Since you are computing from west to east and aren't crossing the International Date Line, there is a five-hour time difference between Rochester and Darby.

puzzle 39
1) dice = pips
2) dots above the "i" = tittle or jot
3) # = octothorpe
4) top of lamp = finial
5) Shoelace tip = aglet

puzzle 40
Might Makes Right

puzzle 41
Place your X in the lower right box. O can't win regardless where they place their next O.

level 1

puzzle 42
Each received two coins because on the walk was a grandfather, who is a son to his mom, the grandfather's son who has a son and is therefore both a father and a son. This makes three people who are both fathers and sons…in this case two fathers and three sons.

puzzle 43
Ohio, Pennsylvania, and Maryland.

puzzle 44
1-c; 2-a; 3-e; 4-b; 5-d

puzzle 45
1) Thailand
2) Argentina
3) Australia
4) Suriname
5) Pakistan

puzzle 46
There are 20 bucks and 10 ducks.

Let A = bucks
B = ducks

A + B = 30
4A + 2B = 100

−2A − 2B = -60
4A + 2B = 100

2A = 40
A = 20
B = 10

puzzle 47
Forty is the only number whose letters are in alphabetical order. The number one is the only number whose letters are in reverse alphabetical order.

puzzle 48
22%. Here's one way to view this:

69 + 21 − 12, who were reading both
= 90 − 12 or 78
100 − 78 = 22 students who were not reading any newspaper.

puzzle 49
m a y pole   f o o t loose
m a y flower   f o o t hills
m a y hem   f o o t bridge

h o r s e power
h o r s e laugh
h o r s e whip

puzzle 50
We found 32. Did you find others?

Nose	Lash	Heel	Calf
Vein	Hair	Brow	Uvea
Nail	Skin	Bone	Fist
Palm	Lung	Axon	Anus
Hand	Back	Knee	Lobe
Foot	Jowl	Nape	Drum
	Neck	Face	
	Chin	Iris	
	Arch	Pore	
	Cell	Head	

puzzle 51
Our spy friend rolled up the map and placed it diagonally in his attaché. It fit nicely, since it formed a triangle that has a hypotenuse of over 5 ft. long:

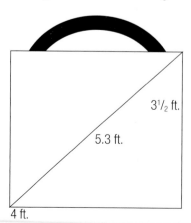

The formula for finding the diagonal is, using the Pythagorean Theorem:
$a^2 + b^2 = c^2$
$(3.5)^2 + 4^2 = c^2$
$12.25 + 16 = c^2$
$c^2 = 28.25$
$c = 5.3$

puzzle 52
G is the letter between and above K and M. M is the letter "just before the letter just above T" and K is the letter "just before the letter just below G." That makes L the letter between K and M – the puzzle asks for the letter just above that, which is G.

puzzle 53
Stand Out In A Crowd

puzzle 54
Don't count your chickens until they are hatched.

puzzle 55
The first number is 3. This is really two sequences in one. Start with the third number in the sequence, which is 8… and look at every other number:

The difference between every other number is 5. Now look at every other number starting with 1.

You can see the difference between these numbers is 5 as well.

puzzle 56

Three days.
She left yesterday and will return tomorrow. If you reasoned she left late yesterday and will return early tomorrow, and therefore will be gone less than 48 hours (and you say that qualifies as two days), that is acceptable as well.

puzzle 57

Wise Beyond His Years

puzzle 58

Too Dumb for Words

puzzle 59

Supercilious

puzzle 60

Two pounds. The two-thirds of a pound of cheese is equivalent to one-third of a block of cheese, so multiply by three to find the whole block:
$3 \times 2/3$ pounds = 2 pounds.

puzzle 61

5/6 of a glass.
Start with a full glass and when you pour out half you then have 1/2 still in the glass. Then pour back in 1/2 of what you poured out, which is 1/4 of a glass. Now the glass is 3/4 full. Then pour out a third of what you now have or 1/3 of 3/4 which equals 1/4 the glass, which means there is 1/2 a glass of water left. Now, pour back in a 1/3 of a glass. So, 1/3 + 1/2 is equal to 5/6 of a glass.

puzzle 62

1-D, 2-A, 3-E, 4-B, 5-C, 6-F.

puzzle 63

2) The blades move counterclockwise.

puzzle 64

22.
$15 \rightarrow 1 \times 1$
$6 \rightarrow 2 \times 2$
$1 \rightarrow 3 \times 3$

puzzle 65

39 cubes. 20 in the large stack on the left and 19 in the large stack on right.

puzzle 66

Bob's friend's name is Molly.

puzzle 67

One th**ou**s**a**nd tw**en**t**y**-fi**ve**

puzzle 68

59
You are looking for the lowest number that is evenly divisible by $2 \times 3 \times 4 \times 5 \times 6$, (which is 720)…and that number is 60. Now you need one less than that for the remainders to fall in sequential order. That number is 59.

puzzle 69

Pool Cues

level 2

puzzle 70
Yes. Your move is to pick up 3 match-sticks. Keep leaving your opponent with a multiple of 4, and you will win.

puzzle 71

1)
A = 9	R = 3
E = 2	S = 8
G = 5	T = 1
L = 4	V = 6
O = 0	

```
    8 0 4 6 2
            9
  + 4 9 3 5 2
  -----------
    1 2 9 8 2 3
```

2)
A = 9	R = 3
E = 2	S = 8
G = 6	T = 1
L = 4	V = 5
O = 0	

```
    8 0 4 5 2
            9
  + 4 9 3 6 2
  -----------
    1 2 9 8 2 3
```

puzzle 72
Shape **C** is the odd one out. The other four shapes can be created without lifting the pencil off the paper, retracing, backtracking or crossing another line.

puzzle 73
Rise to Glory

puzzle 74
480.
 If we exclude the Queen of Diamonds, there are 120 arrangements of the remaining five ($5 \times 4 \times 3 \times 2 \times 1$) cards. The Queen of Diamonds can be inserted in any of the four spaces between the 5 cards; so the answer is four times 120, or 480.

puzzle 75
1) A microsecond is one one-millionth of a second.
2) A Lustrum is five years.
3) A sesquicentennial is every 150 years.
4) Ephemeral is one day.
5) Eon, era, period, epoch.

puzzle 76
5 years old. There are several ways you can solve this. One way is to recognize the multiples of each of the ages:

From the puzzle we know:
cousin = x   brother = 2x   sister = 4x   uncle = 12x

19x equals some number divisible by five and less than 100. The only number that fits is 95.

$19x = 95$ $x = 5$

cousin = 5   brother = 10   sister = 20   uncle = 60

puzzle 77
Square A is 4" × 4"   Square B is 3" × 3"   Square C is 7" × 7"

puzzle 78
1-e; 2-a; 3-d; 4-b; 5-c.

puzzle 79
1) coal   2) Australia   3) December   4) Vulcan

puzzle 80

```
A B C D E F G H I J K L M N O P Q R S T U V W X Y Z
Y Z A B C D E F G H I J K L M N O P Q R S T U V W X
```

Thanks to modern medical advances such as antibiotics, nasal spray, and Diet Coke, it has become routine for people in the civilized world to pass the age of forty, sometimes more than once. –Dave Barry

```
A B C D E F G H I J K L M N O P Q R S T U V W X Y Z
Y D V E K F L B C M G H P O Q Z U I R S W N J A T X
```

In a man's middle years there is scarcely a part of the body he would hesitate to turn over to the proper authorities. –E.B. White

```
A B C D E F G H I J K L M N O P Q R S T U V W X Y Z
Z A B C D E F G H I J K L M N O P Q R S T U V W X Y
```

Inflation is when you pay fifteen dollars for the ten-dollar haircut you used to get for five dollars when you had hair. –Sam Ewing

```
A B C D E F G H I J K L M N O P Q R S T U V W X Y Z
X T D M G K S Q A P R Y I H E U J B Z V N O C D L W
```

When I was younger, I could remember anything, whether it had happened or not; but my faculties are decaying now and soon I shall be so I cannot remember any but the things that never happened. It is sad to go to pieces like this but we all have to do it. – Mark Twain

puzzle 81
1) James Fenimore Cooper wrote The Last of the Mohicans
2) Sid Luckman played football for the Chicago Bears
3) Edvard Munch painted The Scream
4) White Rabbit was a song by Jefferson Airplane
5) Arachnid. A spider has 8 legs and is in the class Arachnid
6) Walter F. Mondale was Vice President under Jimmy Carter
7) Endocrinology. The hypothalamus is part of the endocrine system
8) Venus is the Roman Goddess of Love
9) The Latin prefix for beneath is subter-
10) Fear of being in crowds is enochlophobia. Agoraphobia is also acceptable
11) to, two, and too are homonyms. These are words that sound the same but are spelled differently

puzzle 82
1-c; 2-e; 3-a; 4-b; 5-d

puzzle 83
A Shift In Public Opinion

puzzle 84
Stephen Hawking

puzzle 85
65/99. Here's one way to look at this:

11/13 ★ x = 5/9
(x is the fraction we seek)
11x = 65/9
x = 65/99

puzzle 86
1-d; 2-f; 3-c; 4-a; 5-e; 6-b

puzzle 87
5/7 and 8/9. Take a look at every other fraction starting with 1/3...

1/3   2/4   3/5   4/6...

You can see a pattern of both the numerators and the denominators increasing by one, so the next fraction would be 5/7. Now, look at every other fraction starting with 4/5...

4/5   5/6   6/7   7/8...

Again, both numerator and denominator are increasing by one with each successive fraction. So the next fraction would be 8/9.

puzzle 88
A rolling stone gathers no moss.

puzzle 89
1) The smallest square is 2 × 2.
2) Square A is 11 × 11.

puzzle 90
A) Madame Curie
B) William Shakespeare
C) Bruce Springsteen
D) Clint Eastwood
E) Roger Federer

puzzle 91
196.5 feet per second (about 134 mph). Moving to 90 ft. and having the ball reach home plate in 0.458 seconds, an equation can be set up for x = ft. per sec.

Thus:

90 ft/x = .458 seconds
.458x = 90
x = 90/.458
x = 196.5 ft./second

puzzle 92
Mathematically speaking, no. Out of 8 possibilities, 2 heads come up 3 times. So you have a friend who understands probability. Here are the possibilities in your friend's offer:

H H H   T T T
H H T 1   T T H
H T T   T H H 3
H T H 2   T H T

Your friend has 5/8 of a chance of winning and you only have 3/8 of a chance of winning. Tell him, "No deal!"

puzzle 93
1. UNDERDOG, GROUNDED
2. UNIONS, UNISON
3. TERMINAL, TRAMLINE

puzzle 94
1) 7 wonders of the ancient world
2) 1001 Arabian Nights
3) 12 signs of the zodiac
4) 54 cards in a deck (with jokers)
5) 9 planets in the solar system
6) 88 piano keys
7) 13 stripes on the American flag
8) 32 degrees Fahrenheit at which water freezes
9) 1 day at a time
10) 18 holes on a golf course
11) 90 degrees in a right angle
12) 50 cents in a half dollar
13) 8 sides on a stop sign
14) 3 blind mice (see how they run)
15) 4 quarts in a gallon
16) 24 hours in a day
17) 1 wheel on a unicycle
18) 5 digits in a zip code
19) 57 Heinz varieties
20) 11 players on a football team
21) 7 hills of Rome
22) 101 Dalmatians
23) 64 squares on a chessboard
24) 13 cards in a suit
25) 10 little Indians
26) 20,000 Leagues Under the Sea
27) 13 original colonies
28) 12 knights of the round table
29) 13 in a baker's dozen
30) 66 books of the Bible

puzzle 95
1. Neptune
2. Juno
3. Mars
4. Minerva
5. Mercury
6. Diana

puzzle 96
Figure C is impossible to draw without lifting the pen or pencil to retrace or cross a line.

level 2

puzzle 97
world <u>w i d e</u> spread
place <u>k i c k</u> stand
hard <u>w a r e</u> house
brain <u>c h i l d</u> birth
sweet <u>h e a r t</u> strings
light <u>p r o o f</u> read

puzzle 98
1-d; 2-g; 3-b; 4-c; 5-a; 6-f; 7-e

puzzle 99
82 cents. This would mean one person had 24 cents and the other **57 cents.** When you combine the two, they have 81 cents.

puzzle 100
c. sister-in-law.

puzzle 101
Move any 2 of the 3 numbered matchsticks to...

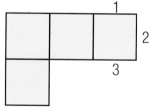

Here:

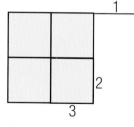

Now you have 5 squares. The 4 small ones and the one large one. We don't care about the extra matchstick sticking out...we don't need it!

puzzle 102
25. The visiting pitcher threw 24 pitches through 8 innings and retired all 24 batters. He then gave up the game-winning home run to the first hitter in the bottom of the ninth. Therefore, he threw 25 total pitches.

puzzle 103
120. When 1/6 left, 5/6 of the people remained. When 2/5 left, 5/6 of 3/5 remained. When 3/4 of the remaining people left, then of 5/6 of 3/5 of 1/4 remained (15/120). Since 15 people were left at the end, there were originally 120 people.

puzzle 104
26.4%. The solution looks like this:

$3/7 \times 11/13 \times 8/11$ = the probability the machines won't fail.

Those three fractions multiplied together = 264/1001 or 26.4 percent.

puzzle 105
Music To One's Ears

puzzle 106
2 2/3 or 2.67. One of the best ways to view this is to set it up as a proportion.

$$\frac{1/_2 \times 9}{6} = \frac{1/_6 \times 12}{?}$$

$4.5 \times ? = 6 \times {}^{12}/_6$

$? = {}^{12}/_{4.5}$

$? = 2{}^2/_3$ or 2.67

puzzle 107
104.

$$\begin{array}{r} 1254 \\ -\ 1150 \\ \hline 104 \end{array}$$

104 divided into each of these numbers leaves a remainder of 6.

puzzle 108
Atmospheric pressure decreases at higher altitudes, so there is much less of it on the water's surface at 10,000 feet. This allows the water to bubble up more quickly, albeit at a lower temperature. Therefore, you'll have to wait longer for your egg to cook.

puzzle 109
Brit ate the cookies.

Look at Bart's statements. Let's say his statement "It was Bret" is true. That means his statement, "It wasn't Bruno" is false. That means it was both Bret and Bruno – a contradiction that cannot be true. This means neither Bret nor Bruno ate the cookies.

Now look at Boone's statements: "It was Brit. It was Bret." We already know it wasn't Bret, so Boone's second statement is false – making his first statement true.

Brit is the culprit.

puzzle 110
Turn both over at the same time. When the three-minute time is done, you have two minutes left in the five-minute timer. Start to mark your seven minute period from here. The instant the two minutes run out, flip the five-minute timer over again to start another five minutes to add onto the two minutes for a total of seven minutes.

puzzle 111
Andre Agassi is the only player to hold all four titles of this group.

puzzle 112
10 ballplayers suffered all 4 injuries. Count the number of ballplayers in each group who did not suffer an injury. Respectively, those numbers are 30, 25, 15, and 20 for a total of 90. Simply subtract this number from 100 and you get 10.

puzzle 113
Pyramid #1 → extraordinarily
Pyramid #2 → impressive

The phrase → extraordinarily
impressive

puzzle 114
Present is the odd one out. All the others have at least one silent letter.

puzzle 115
85. Since we know A + B = Z, it follows that A + B + P = T. Since T + A = F, in the equation B + P + F = 130, replace F with T + A.

B + P + T + A = 130 or B + P + T = 110,
Since A = 20
Rearrange to solve for T:

20 + B + P = T
110 − B − P = T
130 = 2T
65 = T
T + A = F; 65 + 20 = 85
F = 85

puzzle 116
4 to 1.

If P = 3/4 Q, then Q = 4/3 P
If Q = 2/3 R, then R = 3/2 Q
If R = 1/2 S, then S = 2/1 R
Therefore, S to P is 2/1 × 3/2 × 4/3 = 24/6 or 4 to 1.

puzzle 117
72 years old.

Let x be my current age
Then x = 6(x + 6) − 6(x − 6)
x = 6x + 36 − 6x + 36
x = 72 years old.

puzzle 118
100 pounds of the $36 chemical and 50 pounds of the $48 chemical.

Set up two equations, with x as the $48 chemical and y as the $36 chemical:

1) x + y = 150, or x = 150 − y
2) 48x + 36y = 150 x 40

Substituting in equation 2), we have:

48(150 − y) + 36y = 6,000
7200 − 48y + 36y = 6,000
12y = 1,200
y = 100
Since x + y = 150
x = 50

puzzle 119
1) Julius Caesar
2) The Boston Tea Party
3) Silence of the Lambs
4) Winston Churchill
5) Serena Williams
6) Pulitzer Prize
7) The Grateful Dead

puzzle 120

puzzle 121
20 pages of 900 words and 20 pages of 1500 words.
Here's one way to view this:

1) 900x + 1500y = 48,000
2) x + y = 40
3) x = 40 − y
4) Substituting, 900(40 − y) + 1500y = 48,000
5) 36,000 − 900y + 1500y = 48,000
6) 600y = 12,000
7) y = 20, therefore, x = 20

level 2

puzzle 122

Three. We're talking about the number of times the letter "a" appears in each animal's name.

puzzle 123

"Cowards die many times before their deaths; The valiant never taste of death but once."

puzzle 124

Second String

puzzle 125

1)

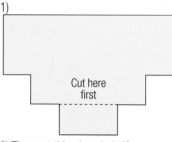

2) Then cut this piece in half:

3) Then place the 2 small pieces as shown here:

puzzle 126

1. ade, aid, aide
2. ads, adds, adze
3. air, err, heir
4. ait, ate, eight
5. aye, eye, I
6. axel, axil, axle
7. bailer, bailor, baler
8. baize, bays, beys
9. bald, balled, bawled
10. bases, basis, basses
11. beau, bo, bow
12. bel, bell, belle
13. bight, bite, byte
14. birr, bur, burr
15. boar, boor, bore
16. bold, bolled, bowled
17. bole, boll, bowl
18. borough, burro, burrow
19. bourn, born, borne
20. braise, brays, braze
21. brews, brewis, bruise
22. bused, bussed, bust
23. buy, by, bye
24. cain, cane, kain
25. call, caul, col
26. cay, key, quay
27. cees, seas, sees, seize
28. caret, carrot, karat
29. cedar, ceder, seeder
30. ceiling, sealing, seeling
31. censer, censor, sensor,
32. cere, sear, seer, sere
33. chord, cored, cord
34. cinque, sink, sync, synch
35. cite, sight, site
36. cited, sighted, sited
37. coal, cole, kohl
38. coarse, corse, course
39. coign, coin, quoin
40. coolie, coolly, coulee
41. crew, cru, krewe, crewe
42. crews, cruise, cruse, kruse
43. dieing, dyeing, dying
44. do, dew, due
45. does, dos, doughs, doze
46. earn, ern, erne, urn
47. ewe, yew, you
48. ewes, use, yews
49. fain, fane, feign
50. faro, farrow, pharoah
51. eau, o, oh, owe
52. fays, faze, phase
53. firs, furs, furze
54. flew, flu, flue
55. for, fore, four
56. fraise, frays, phrase
57. frees, freeze, frieze
58. gild, gilled, guild
59. gnus, news, nus
60. hi, hie, high
61. hoard, horde, whored
62. holey, holy, wholly
63. idle, idol, idyll
64. knows, noes, nose
65. lais, lase, lays, laze, leis
66. lea, lee, li
67. lear, leer, lehr
68. liar, lier, lyre
69. lode, load, lowed
70. maize, maze, mays
71. marc, mark, marque
72. marri, marry, merry
73. meat, meet, mete
74. moor, more, mohrr
75. nay, nee, neigh
76. need, knead, kneed
77. new, knew, gnu
78. not, knot, naught
79. oar, or, ore
80. pallet, palate, palette
81. peak, peek, pique
82. pearl, perle (pearle), purl
83. peace, piece, peise
84. polar, poler, poller
85. praise, prays, preys
86. psi, sigh, xi
87. raise, rays, raze
88. raiser, razer, razor
89. rain, reign, rein
90. rapped, rapt, wrapped
91. read, red, redd
92. read, rede, reed
93. rei, rye, wry
94. reis, rise, ryes
95. right, rite, write, wright
96. rhos, roes, rose, rows
97. road, rode, rowed
98. rood, rude, rued
99. roomie, roomy, rheumy
100. sacks, sacs, sax
101. senate, sennet, sennit
102. sew, so, sow

103. shire, shier, shyer
104. sighs, size, psis
105. sign, sine, syne
106. slew, slough, slue
107. sold, soled, souled
108. tael, tail, tale,
109. tare, ter, tear
110. tea, tee, ti
111. tease, tees, tes
112. tern, terne, turn
113. to, too, two
114. toad, toed, towed
115. vail, vale, veil
116. vial, vile, viol
117. wail, wale, whale
118. way, weigh, whey
119. whined, wind, wined, wynd

puzzle 127
The resulting figure will look like figure D

puzzle 128
It is 8:00 p.m.
8 hours ago it was noon.
6 hours later it would be 6:00 p.m.
18 hours of the day have passed by 6:00 p.m., which is ¾ of the day.

puzzle 129
1-B; 2-C; 3-D; 4-A.

puzzle 130
1) Ventral
2) Supinate
3) 4
4) 5 to 3
5) Walker Cup

puzzle 131
1) Oscar Wilde
2) Theodor Geisel (Dr. Seuss)
3) Allen Ginsburg
4) Ernest Hemingway
5) Charles Dickens

puzzle 132
Tennessee is the other state.

puzzle 133
3. The sums of the diagonals are equal.]

About
Terry Stickels

Author and speaker Terry Stickels dedicates his life to helping improve mental flexibility and creative problem solving skills while making it fun. His books, calendars, card decks, and newspaper columns contain clever and challenging puzzles that stretch the minds of even the best thinkers.

Terry's first puzzle column appeared in a 12-newspaper syndicate in Rochester, New York in 1992. Two years later his first book *MINDSTRETCHING PUZZLES*, Sterling Publishing, was released. Twenty-nine puzzle books followed.

Not only are Terry's books used for enjoyment worldwide, but organizations like the National Council of Teachers of Mathematics praise his work as important in assisting students to learn to think critically.

Terry's popularity spread to three nationally-syndicated columns. *FRAME GAMES*™ and *Stickdoku*™ appear in *USA WEEKEND* Magazine read by over 48 million people in 600 newspapers weekly. *STICKELERS* (sic) puzzle column is distributed by King Features in over 200 daily newspapers. His puzzles have appeared on Kellogg's Raisin Bran cereal boxes and on the Universal Studios website featuring the 2001 movie *A Beautiful Mind*. *New York Times* crossword editor Will Shortz has used Terry's puzzles on his *NPR Weekend Edition* Sunday morning segment.

Terry is also a popular public speaker. His presentations are fast paced, humorous looks at the ability, and sometimes lack thereof, to think clearly. Using puzzles, he engages audiences in interactive fun as he helps them discover the hidden power of their minds.

He attended the University of Nebraska at Omaha on a football scholarship. While tutoring math and physics, he used puzzles as a non-intimidating way to improve thinking skills.

You can find out more about Terry Stickels' puzzles at www.terrystickels.com.

PUBLISHER
Richard Fraiman
GENERAL MANAGER
Steven Sandonato
EXECUTIVE DIRECTOR, MARKETING SERVICES
Carol Pittard
DIRECTOR, RETAIL & SPECIAL SALES
Tom Mifsud
DIRECTOR, NEW PRODUCT DEVELOPMENT
Peter Harper
ASSISTANT DIRECTOR, BOOKAZINE MARKETING
Laura Adam
**ASSISTANT PUBLISHING DIRECTOR,
BRAND MARKETING**
Joy Butts
ASSOCIATE COUNSEL
Helen Wan
ASSOCIATE MANAGER, PRODUCT MARKETING
Nina Fleishman
BRAND & LICENSING MANAGER
Alexandra Bliss
DESIGN & PREPRESS MANAGER
Anne-Michelle Gallero
ASSISTANT PRODUCTION MANAGER
Brynn Joyce

DESIGN AND PRODUCTION
Symbology Creative
Mark Wainwright

SPECIAL THANKS:
Christine Austin
Glenn Buonocore
Jim Childs
Susan Chodakiewicz
Rose Cirrincione
Jacqueline Fitzgerald
Lauren Hall
Jennifer Jacobs
Suzanne Janso
Mona Li
Robert Marasco
Amy Migliaccio
Brooke Reger
Dave Rozzelle
Ilene Schreider
Adriana Tierno
Alex Voznesenskiy
Sydney Webber

PUZZLES CREATED BY TERRY STICKELS

All puzzles and accompanying illustrations
in this book © 2009 Terry Stickels

FRAME GAMES is a registered trademark of Terry Stickels

alzheimer's ℞ association®

About the Alzheimer's Association
The Alzheimer's Association is the leading voluntary health organization in Alzheimer care, support and research. Our mission is to eliminate Alzheimer's disease through the advancement of research; to provide and enhance care and support for all affected; and to reduce the risk of dementia through the promotion of brain health.

Alzheimer's Association National Office
225 N. Michigan Ave., Fl. 17
Chicago, IL 60601
24/7 information and referral 1.800.272.3900 and www.alz.org.